What's Her Name

What's Her Name

By Tomac Scott
Illustrated by Casey Pardue

Tomac Scott

Copyright © 2018 by Tomac Scott

All rights reserved. No portion of this publication may be reproduced, stored in a retrieval system, or transmitted by any means-electronic, mechanical, photocopying, recording, or any other-except for brief quotations in printed reviews, without the prior written permission of the author.

This book is a work of fiction. Names, characters, places, and incidents either are products of the author's imagination or are used fictitiously. Any resemblance to actual events or persons, living or dead, is entirely coincidental.

Illustrator: Casey Pardue

Executive Editor: Regina Cornell

Layout: 3SIXTY Marketing Studio - www.3sixtyprinting.com

Indigo River Publishing
3 West Garden Street Ste. 352
Pensacola, FL 32502
www.indigoriverpublishing.com

Ordering Information:

Quantity sales: Special discounts are available on quantity purchases by corporations, associations, and others. For details, contact the publisher at the address above.

Orders by U.S. trade bookstores and wholesalers: Please contact the publisher at the address above.

Printed in the United States of America

Library of Congress Control Number: 2018949206

ISBN: 978-1-948080-75-0

First Edition

With Indigo River Publishing, you can always expect great books, strong voices, and meaningful messages. Most importantly, you'll always find…words worth reading.

I would like to extend a special thank you to Shiela Niles, Kenyan Nygera, Lisa, and Shayla Scott. I love you all. Thank you to everyone that has supported my book. I look forward to sharing more stories with you in the future.

Bunu (Boo-New) is moving to a new town with her mother today. She already misses her old friends, but she is ready to make new ones.

In the morning, Bunu was so excited to make new friends that she packed her own lunch and ran out before her mother was even ready!

"Hello, class. Today we have a new student. Can you tell us your name?" The teacher asked.

"Hi, I'm Bunu!"

...She didn't mean to yell, but she was so excited.

There was a long silence...

"She said her name is Boo-Boo!" One of the kids called out and the whole class laughed.

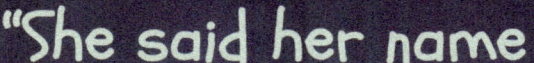

When Bunu walked to her seat she heard some of the kids making fun of her...

Bunu sat by herself at lunch. The kids were not as nice as the ones at her old school.

When she opened her lunchbox, all her food was bad!

When Bunu got home,
her mother asked how her day was.

Bunu started to cry.

"All of the kids are so mean!
Why is my name so weird?
No one likes it."

Her mother hugged her
and dried her tears.

"...My grandmother was from a small village in India. She was so beautiful that one day the prince brought an artist to paint her. The prince even wanted to marry her.

She fell in love with the artist instead. She turned down a prince to be with your grandfather. You are just as strong and beautiful as she was. That is why I named you after her." The story made Bunu feel a lot better.

Bunu felt happy and confident after hearing about how strong her Grandmother was. She was determined to try and make friends and stayed up with her mother to make cupcakes for the kids at school the next day.

On the bus the next day she met a new friend from her class.

"Hi, Bunu!

I'm Vince.

Do you want to sit with me at lunch?"

"Sure!"

Bunu got to class early so that she could give everyone the cupcakes she had baked.

Most of the kids were grateful, but some of them laughed and called them "Boo-Boo" cakes.

Bunu was sad that some of her classmates still made fun of her, but she was excited to sit with Vince at lunch. A couple new friends even came to sit with them!
"Hi, Bunu! My name's Ashley. Thanks for the cupcakes!"
"Yeah, they are really good! I'm Jason."

Bunu sat with Ashley, Vince, and Jason for the rest of the lunch period! They told her not to worry about those other mean kids. They were just haters, and her new friends were sure that the other kids would see how cool and fun she was soon! Bunu felt a lot better about herself and she went home with a **big smile on her face.**

Bunu was so happy and she made so many new friends that day!
She made even more great friends as the week passed and fewer and fewer kids made fun of her.

Sometimes the mean kids bothered her, but she knew that people loved her and that she just had to keep being herself.

That weekend, Bunu went to the mall with her mom and ran into her new friends. There was a company looking for kids to star in commercials for a fashion agency. Bunu wasn't too sure, but her friends encouraged her to tryout.

"Hi, I'm Bunu."
She told the interviewer.
"Wow, that's a really unique name!"
"It was my great-grandmother's name. She was really cool, and my mom named me after her."

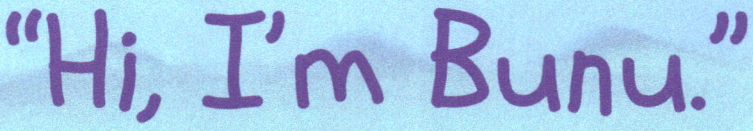

They wanted her to star in the commercial and they even wanted to use her name! Soon, her name was appearing all over town!

All of the kids were so happy for her! They were so excited about the name "Bunu" now and nobody made fun of her name anymore! Bunu knew then just how special she was to have a unique name.

She knew that sometimes people would be mean and make fun of her for being different, but she would never let that make her sad again.

She was proud to be Bunu!

 Tomac Scott is a jet mechanic and military veteran from Cleveland, Ohio. During his childhood, he was bullied and taunted because of his unusual name. Over the years, he discovered the lasting effects that bullying can have on children like himself. Through his writing, he aims to help today's youth overcome the same challenges that he faced as a child. The biggest and most important lesson he learned was that you have to show bullies that they have no influence over your life.

By staying positive and continuing to be yourself, the bullies will stop because they see something in you that they do not have themselves.

Bunu

To: AVA-MONET

TO: AVA-MONET

CPSIA information can be obtained
at www.ICGtesting.com
Printed in the USA
BVHW022019181019
561508BV00010B/18/P